# Day-by-Day
# 100th Day Activities

## Quick & Fun Math Activities for Counting Up to the 100th Day of School

by Charlotte Sassman
and Deborah Diffily

SCHOLASTIC
PROFESSIONAL BOOKS

New York • Toronto • London • Auckland • Sydney
Mexico City • New Delhi • Hong Kong • Buenos Aires

Cover design by Norma Ortiz
Interior design by Holly Grundon
Cover art by Stacy Lamb
Interior art by Teresa Anderko
Interior photographs by Deborah Diffily and Charlotte Sassman

ISBN 0-439-32068-2

# Contents

# Introduction

Keeping track of the number of school days and celebrating the 100th day are popular activities in early childhood classrooms. Rather than just noting the number of each day, learning experiences related to counting the days can be incorporated into class routines. The activities in this book do just that.

For each number, 1-100, brief activities enrich and extend children's understanding of mathematical concepts. The activities support the many ways young children learn best. They suggest ways to help children connect numbers to things in their world. Most activities call for movement and action on the part of each child. Children will move, write, draw, paint, play, create, observe, think, share, and sing as they explore numbers and make connections between numbers and their lives.

Activities are organized in sets of ten—nine days of short activities and a celebration for each tenth day of school. Four of the celebration activities follow the pattern of providing children with opportunities to play, do, read, and make something related to the number of the day, and one activity repeats the same task (stringing cereal). Repeating this task every ten days helps children develop an understanding of how larger numbers represent larger quantities.

Working through these quick and easy activities does more for your class than just teach simple math concepts. As you model target skills—for example, correctly writing numerals on the chalkboard—you are setting the standard for the class's work. And as you remark about the number of legs on a spider or hours in a day, you are introducing concepts and ideas that will be studied later in more detail.

Offer children time to discover the relationships between the activities they are doing and the number of the day. Questioning children about what they see is important to their learning. For example, on Day 6 call the names of six children and ask them to stand. Ask: "Why are just these children standing?" Some children will make the connection between the circle activity and the numeral, noting that the day's number is 6.

## Bulletin Board Ideas

❁ Create a number line in the classroom by adding one number each day. It can resemble a caterpillar that begins with a large circle, labeled "1," hung on the first day of school. Every day of school thereafter, add one more circle labeled with the next number. By the hundredth day of school, the caterpillar stretches around the room, with each section of the insect showing a number 1-100!

❦ Your number line can also be as simple as sticky notes (hung one per day). By using different-colored notes, you are color-coding the number line to reinforce different counting concepts. (Every other number could be written on different colors, so that even numbers are one color and odd numbers another color. The color of the sticky notes could be changed every ten days to help children "see" groups of ten. Or, all numbers could be the same color, with the exception of multiples of 5 and 10, to help children learn to count by 5's or 10's.)

❁ Start a "10's Bulletin Board" on the Celebrate 10 Day. As a class, count 10 cotton balls, place them in a reclosable bag, and hang it on the wall. On the Celebrate 20 Day, repeat the activity with 20 cotton balls. Repeat on each Celebration Day. Hanging these bags in a column or row allows children to "see" the difference between larger numbers of items.

## Days 1-9

### Supply List

number cubes (1 per child)

8 markers or crayons in a box

### Vocabulary

count

number cube

grid

number

pattern

square

triangle

### About Days 1-9

Young children are often encouraged to hold up fingers to show how old they are. So we suggest introducing numbers to young children by asking them to do just this—raise fingers to "show numbers." Each of the first nine days starts this way. After this introduction, clap the number, model writing it, ask the children to "write" the number in the air, then show that number of things to the group. By participating in these repeating activities for Days 1-9, the children will connect numbers to something they already know and extend that knowledge.

Spending the first few days of school repeating the same sequence of activities establishes a routine for children. It also offers opportunities for children to practice following simple oral directions.

Remember, when you write numerals in the air for the children, form them backward so the children (who are facing you) see them formed correctly.

## Day 1

❀ Hold up 1 finger. Ask children to clap 1 time, in unison.

❁ Write the numeral 1 on the chalkboard or chart paper.

❀ Ask children to join in as you write a 1 in the air. They can also use their pointer finger to write a 1 on the floor. (Suggest that they "smooth out"

6

a piece of "pretend paper" on the floor and "write" on it with their pointer finger. The pretend paper can always be "erased" with a wipe of the hand and the numeral can be rewritten.)

🌷 Call 1 child's name and ask him or her to go get 1 pencil and bring it to the circle.

# Day 2

👦 Hold up 2 fingers. Ask children to show their 2 arms, 2 eyes, 2 ears, 2 legs, and 2 feet.

👧 Ask children to slap each thigh, in turn, until 2 slaps have been made. (First touch the right hand to the right thigh and then repeat with the left hand and left thigh to make 2 slaps.)

👦 Write the numeral 2 on the chalkboard. Remark that there are 2 wings on a bird and 2 wheels on a bicycle. Ask children to join in as you write a 2 in the air, or to use their pointer finger to write a 2 on the floor.

In addition to these circle-time activities, incorporate number concepts into daily conversation, center activities, and your structured math lessons.

# Day 3

✏️ Hold up 3 fingers.

⭐ Clap 3 times, in unison.

✏️ Show a large drawing of a triangle. Count the sides and the points.

⭐ Write a 3 on the chalkboard. Remark that there are 3 wheels on a tricycle and 3 lights on a stoplight. Ask children to join in as you write a 3 in the air, and to use their pointer finger to write a 3 on the floor.

The numeral 3 is often reversed by young children. Emphasize the numeral's starting point and forward-moving direction. Indicate that the "pencil moves up and forward before coming around."

# Day 4

🐱 Hold up 4 fingers.

🐶 Ask children to alternately slap each thigh, in turn, until 4 slaps have been made. Have them count aloud as you slap each thigh.

🐱 Show a large drawing of a square. Count the sides and the points.

🐶 Write a 4 on the chalkboard. Remark that there are 4 wheels on a car. Ask children to join in as you write a 4 in the air, or to use their pointer finger to write a 4 on the floor.

# Day 5

✏️ Hold up 5 fingers. Match the fingertips of one hand to the fingertips of the opposite hand. (Young children often find this difficult. Help them by modeling how to begin with joining the thumbs, and moving on to one finger at a time. Or, have them begin with the pinkie finger and move on to the rest.)

❤️ Clap 5 times, in unison.

✏️ Sketch a 5-pointed star on the chalkboard and count the points. Show the dot pattern on a number cube for 5, sketching it on the chalkboard as children count the dots.

❤️ Write a 5 on the chalkboard. Ask children to join in as you write a 5 in the air, or to use their pointer finger to write a 5 on the floor.

# Day 6

✿ Hold up 6 fingers. Remark that it takes both hands to hold up 6 fingers.

🌷 Ask children to slap each thigh, in turn, until 6 slaps have been made. Have them count aloud as they slap each thigh.

✿ Write the numeral 6 on the chalkboard. Ask children to join in as you write a 6 in the air. Remark that there are 6 legs on an insect. Ask children to use their pointer finger to write a 6 on the floor.

🌷 Choose 6 children and ask them to stand up. In unison, count the children who are standing.

# Day 7

☺ Hold up 7 fingers.

☺ Clap 7 times, in unison.

☺ Note that there are 7 days in a week. Sing the song, "There are 7 Days" (to the tune of "Found a Peanut"):

There are 7 days, there are 7 days,
There are 7 days in a week.
Sunday, Monday,
Tuesday, Wednesday,
Thursday, Friday, Saturday.

☺ Write a 7 on the chalkboard. Ask children to join in as you write a 7 in the air, or to use their pointer finger to write a 7 on the floor.

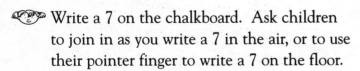

# Day 8

✏️ Hold up 8 fingers.

⭐ Ask children to slap each thigh, in turn, until 8 slaps have been made. Count aloud as you slap each thigh.

✏️ Write the numeral 8 on the chalkboard. Ask children to join in as you write an 8 in the air. Remark that there are 8 legs on a spider. Ask children to use their pointer finger to write an 8 on the floor.

✨ Show a box of 8 felt-tip markers or crayons. Have children count them as you hold them up, one by one.

In advance, collect empty egg cartons for the activity on Day 12. Each child will need a carton. Request donations in a family letter or post a request outside the classroom door.

# Day 9

🐱 Hold up 9 fingers.

🐶 Clap 9 times, in unison.

🐱 Write a 9 on the chalkboard. Ask children to join in as you write a 9 in the air, or to use their pointer finger to write a 9 on the floor.

🐶 Remark that there are 9 players on a baseball team. Have children count the players as you name the positions — pitcher, catcher, first base, second base, third base, shortstop, left field, center field, and right field.

10

# Celebrate 10 Day

## Supply List

yarn

0-shaped cereal

upholstery needles

small objects, such as beans, cubes, pennies, or buttons

Unifix® cubes

self-adhesive dots

2 X 5 grids (1 per child)

crayons

Read
*Ten Black Dots*
by Donald
Crews

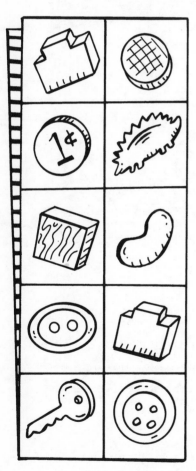

## Number Necklace:

Provide small bowls of round cereal (such as Cheerios® or Froot Loops®) and a length of yarn or string for each child. Challenge children to string exactly 10 pieces of cereal to make a necklace. Later, children can eat the cereal.

**Play:** Provide pairs of children with reclosable bags containing 10 Unifix® cubes. Ask children to snap the cubes together to make a tower. Alternately, children can stack 10 blocks, or join 10 Multi-Links® to make a creature.

**Do:** Provide children with a 2- by 5-square grid made on a piece of paper (see left). Have each child fill in the grid with 10 objects.

Help children use long, blunt needles to string the cereal. These needles are often sold in arts and crafts stores as tapestry or upholstery needles. Alternately, wrap a small piece of clear tape on the end of the yarn to make it stiff enough to go through the cereal. Cut the yarn and thread the needles before class.

**Make:** Give children crayons and 10 self-sticking dots each and let them use the dots to make any kind of picture they wish. Bind the pages together to create a class book.

## Days 11-19

### Vocabulary

connect

cubes

dozen

inch

longer/
shorter

measuring

nickel

one-to-one
correspon-
dence

penny

rods

skip counting

sorting

square

### Supply List

| | |
|---|---|
| an egg carton for each child | reclosable bags |
| 15 pennies and 3 nickels per child | ice cube tray |
| Chess game | Checkers game |
| small manipulatives such as cereal, buttons, marbles, and keys | toy tractor-trailer truck (with 18 wheels) |

### About Days 11-19

Young children often have trouble learning to rote count from 11 to 19. These numbers do not have the same oral pattern that starts with the 20's. Just as "The Alphabet Song" helps many children learn to recite the letters of the alphabet, "Number Rock" (Greg and Steve, *We All Live Together*, Volume 2) helps children rote count from 1 to 20.

The activities for Days 11-19 continue to focus on counting, with an emphasis on connecting numbers to real things in the children's lives: a football team, a dozen eggs, the games of checkers and chess, and 18-wheelers.

# Day 11

Draw 11 O's to show a football team's formation. Explain that this is one way a coach tells players how to run different plays. Ask children to count the number of players on the team with you. Talk about how 11 is a "twin number"—having a 1 in the 10's place and a 1 in the 1's place. Model writing the number 11, and have children practice writing 11 in the air.

O  O  O  O  O  O

O  O                    O

O  O

Show children the formation of a football team.

# Day 12

Give every child an empty egg carton and a reclosable bag containing 12 items. Demonstrate counting items as you place one in each section, then lead children through counting items 1-12. Discuss the word "dozen." As an alternate activity, use 12 cookies as an example of a dozen.

You might also use plastic eggs to fill each section in the carton. First, have the children count the eggs, then sections in the carton. Remark about the one-to-one correspondence between the eggs and the sections.

There are 12 red and 12 black game pieces used in the game of Checkers. Children may already know how to play and can count the game pieces as they set up the board.

# Day 13

🌼 Remind children about the word *dozen* and ask them to recall how many are in a dozen. Then explain the idea of a baker's dozen, which is 12 plus one more—an extra roll is the baker's way of saying thank you to the customer. Draw an illustration of a baker's dozen of donuts, asking children to count as you draw. Draw circles and count from 1 to 13. Write 13 beside your drawing and lead children in writing 13 in the air.

# Day 14

🌷 Freeze water in an ice cube tray to make 14 ice cubes (standard ice cube trays are arranged in rows with 7 cubes on each side). Pop them out of the tray, asking the children to count to 14 with you. Alternately, place a small manipulative in each space in the tray, asking children to count aloud to 14.

# Day 15

🌼 Prepare reclosable bags containing 15 pennies and 3 nickels for each child. Lead children as they lay out a 3-by-5 array as they count 15 pennies. Then introduce skip counting, counting by 5's. After practicing counting by 5's a few times, explain that a nickel is worth the same as 5 pennies. Demonstrate counting the 3 nickels by 5's.

# Day 16

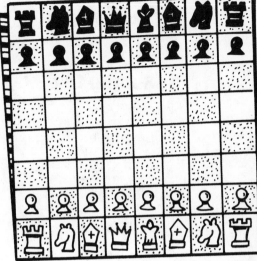

Show a Chess board and count the game pieces, or show a picture of a Chess board ready for play. (Chess uses 16 pieces on each side of the board. The pieces are arranged in 2 rows of 8 each.)

# Day 17

Cut pieces of yarn or string to 17 inches long. Distribute the yarn to children, asking them to find one thing in the room shorter than 17 inches and one thing longer than 17 inches. Can they find anything that is exactly 17 inches?

# Day 18

Show a toy tractor-trailer truck or sketch a large truck with 18 wheels. Point to the wheels as children count them.

# Day 19

Ask small groups of children to sort a bag of items by type (create several collections of 19 from an assortment of small items—like buttons, keys, nuts, bolts, pebbles, or coins—and store them in gallon-sized reclosable bags) and then talk about their sorting strategies. Discuss the different number combinations that equal 19.

## Celebrate 20 Day

Read
*One Moose,
Twenty Mice*
by Clare
Beaton

### Supply List

| | |
|---|---|
| yarn | number cubes |
| paper plates | Unifix® cubes |
| O-shaped cereal | small manipulatives (20 per child) |
| upholstery needles | copies of page 55 (1 per child) |

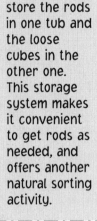

Store the Unifix® cubes in two large plastic tubs. After children build the rods, store the rods in one tub and the loose cubes in the other one. This storage system makes it convenient to get rods as needed, and offers another natural sorting activity.

**Play:** Play the math game "20's." Each pair of players needs a paper plate, 20 small objects, and a number cube (these items store easily in a gallon-sized reclosable bag). The first player rolls, then moves that number of objects onto the plate. The other player rolls, adding that number of objects to the plate. Play continues until 20 objects are on the plate.

**Do:** Give each child a copy of the reproducible on page 55. Instruct them to color in the two wheels on each bicycle.

**Make:** Invite children to use two colors of Unifix® cubes to build two rods with 10 cubes each. Children can then connect their two rods to make 20. All the rods in the class can be connected and counted by 2's (or 20's)!

## Days 21 - 29

### Supply List

| | |
|---|---|
| Unifix® cubes | calendar |
| yarn | reclosable bags |
| pennies, nickels, and quarters | photographs of buttercups, irises, wild roses, black-eyed Susans, and asters |

### About Days 21-29

Learning the rote counting of 21-29 is a bit easier for children because these numbers all start with "twenty-". This is a good time to introduce the Hundred Chart (page 54) to the class. Use a pointer to point to each number during the count up to each day's number.

Skip counting by 5's, dozens, and the number of players on a football team are repeated in this section. New concepts of time and the calendar are introduced, as well as counting items connected to science concepts (petals on a flower, bones in the hand).

This section also introduces activities that can be used for any day. You can always substitute a lesson with one of the following activities:

- Have a reclosable bag with a certain number of blocks ready for circle time. Spill the contents in the middle of the circle and ask children how many blocks are in the pile. After several guesses, ask how the blocks could be arranged to be counted more easily. One way could be to make rows of 5, then count by 5's, then by 1's.

- Cut a piece of yarn or string a certain number of inches long. Have children find one thing in the class shorter than the yarn and one thing longer than the yarn.

- Give each child a book. Count the pages aloud, as children turn the pages.

### Vocabulary

calendar

clock

double/single

hours

leap year

month

quarter

same/ different

twin numbers

# Day 21

🐱 Explain to children that different types of flowers have different numbers of petals. Display a photograph of a lily or an iris, and tell children that these flowers always have 3 petals. Show a photograph of a butter-cup or a wild rose, and tell children that these flowers always have 5 petals. Finally, present an aster or a black-eyed Susan, noting that these flowers always have 21 petals. Draw an aster and label the petals as children count from 1 to 21.

# Day 22

🐶 Draw 11 X's and 11 O's to show two football teams' formations (right). Remind children that this is the way a coach tells players how to run different plays. Ask them to count the number of players on each team with you. Model writing the twin number 22, and have children practice writing 22 in the air.

🐱 Use this day to introduce "doubles" to your class, such as 1+1, 2+2, 3+3, and so on. Review "doubles" up to 11+11. Using Unifix® cubes, show the class one rod of 10 and a single cube. Ask them to tell what number the cubes represent together. Show another rod of 10 and 1 cube and model putting the 2 groups of cubes together. Count to 22.

# Day 23

✎ Have a reclosable bag of 23 Unifix® cubes ready for circle time. Spill the contents in the middle of the circle and ask children how many cubes there are in the pile. After several guesses, ask how the cubes could be arranged to count them more easily. One way could be making rows of 5, then counting by 5's, then by 1's (5, 10, 15, 20, 21, 22, 23).

# Day 24

♥ Remind children about counting to 12 (one dozen), as they did on Day 12. Discuss how two dozen cookies would make 24 cookies. Children can count the cookies as you draw them on the board.

✎ Show a clock, counting 24 hours for one day. (A Judy Clock® works well for this activity.)

# Day 25

♥ Provide pairs of children with a reclosable bag containing 25 pennies. Encourage them to count the pennies by arranging them into groups of 5. Explain that a quarter is worth 25 cents and 5 nickels also equal 25 cents. Ask them what they might buy with a quarter.

# Day 26

Ask children if they can think of anything with 26 parts. Give hints so that someone guesses the alphabet. Hints might include: "We write some of them every day"; "Sometimes we sing them"; "The name Carlos has 6 of them." When a child says, "the alphabet," point to the alphabet chart in the classroom and count the number of letters together.

# Day 27

There are 27 bones in our hands! Provide a sketch of the bones in a hand for the children to see. (You can enlarge the sketch at right or draw your own.) Color in the bones as children count them. Children can trace around their hand and sketch in the bones, following the model you show. Encourage them to label the bones with numerals as they count them.

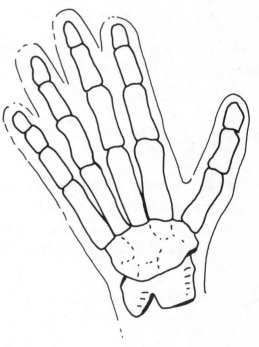

# Day 28

Show the class a February calendar. Count the days in the month together. Why is February different from other months?

# Day 29

Explain that February is the only month where the number of days that it has changes. Show a calendar from a leap year and count the number of days in it. (In leap year, the Gregorian calendar has 366 days, with the extra day inserted to compensate for the quarter-day difference between an ordinary year and the astronomical year.)

Read
*Let's Count*
by Tana
Hoban

## Celebrate 30 Day

### Supply List

| | |
|---|---|
| yarn | craft sticks |
| upholstery needles | squares of cardboard |
| 4 plastic tubs | square napkins |
| Goldfish® or similar snack | copies of page 56 (1 per child) |
| 0-shaped cereal | red, yellow, and green crayons |

**Number Necklace:** Provide small bowls of cereal and a length of yarn or string for each child. As children string exactly 30 pieces of cereal on the necklaces, note that they are getting longer. Later, children can eat the cereal.

**Play:** Place 4 tubs in the front of the room. Label 3 of them as "10" and the other tub as "left overs." Ask children to each gather 2 small objects from the room and return to the circle area. Fill the first tub with 10 objects, counting aloud from 1-10. Then, fill the other two tubs with 10 objects. Place the "left over" objects in the last tub. Recount the objects, emphasizing that 3 groups of 10 makes 30.

**Do:** Give the children a copy of page 56 and invite them to color the lights on each traffic signal and write the number of lights in all.

**Make:** Glue 10 popsicle sticks flat to cardboard. Glue 10 more on top of those, going the opposite direction. Glue 10 more on top, going the first direction. After these creations dry, they can be used as platters for a snack, holding 30 small crackers or something equally small. (Place a napkin on the popsicle stick creation so the glue doesn't get on the snack.)

## Days 31 - 39

### Supply List

| | |
|---|---|
| calendar | yardstick |
| thermometer | 36 1-inch blocks |
| Unifix® cubes | books with at least 37 pages |
| sentence strips | pairs of socks |
| nickels | paper plates |
| reclosable bags | |

### Vocabulary

- columns/ rows
- degrees
- edge
- estimate
- Fahrenheit
- faster
- inches
- pair
- parallel
- pattern
- slower
- thermometer
- yard
- yardstick

## About Days 31-39

This section builds on previous activities with the calendar, using Unifix® cubes to represent numbers, and skip counting by 5's. It also introduces new concepts of temperature, a yardstick, skip counting by 2's, and using manipulatives to solve problems. Continue to use the 100's chart so children can see the patterns involved in counting.

## Day 31

✐ Display the calendar pages for January, March, May, July, August, October, and December. Ask children to discover what they all have in common. Lead children into looking for the last day of each month. Choose one month and count the days together.

## Day 32

☆ Show children a weather thermometer. Explain that 32 degrees Fahrenheit is the temperature at which water freezes. Count the degrees from 1 to 32. You might even pass around an ice cube!

## Day 33

✐ Using Unifix® cubes, build enough 10-cube rods and singles (1's) to make 33. Count to 33. Model adding 11+11+11=33.

☆ Model writing the twin number 33, and have children practice writing 33 in the air.

> In advance, ask children to bring old or mismatched pairs of clean socks to be used on Day 38.

# Day 34

🐱 Sing the song "Supercalifragilisticexpialidocious"! Write the word on the board, and lead children in counting the letters of this very, very long word! Or write the word on a sentence strip, roll it up and then slowly unroll it as you say the word.

# Day 35

🐶 Give pairs of children resealable bags containing 7 nickels each. Lead them into counting by 5's to 35. Then, rote count from 1 to 35. Ask children which way of counting is faster, and which way is slower. Focus on the vocabulary words *faster* and *slower*.

Ask families to help collect "45 cents off" coupons to use on Day 45.

# Day 36

🐱 Show a yardstick and bag of 1-inch blocks to the class. (Have at least 36 blocks in the bag.) Ask them to estimate how many blocks it would take to make a line as long as the yardstick. Record several estimates. Then ask two children to make a line of blocks parallel to the yardstick, and have the class count aloud as each square is added. Finally, see which estimate was the closest. Explain that 36 inches equals a yard.

🐶 Use 36 cookies as an example of 3 dozen.

# Day 37

🐱 Give each child a book. Count the pages 1-37 aloud, as children turn the pages.

# Day 38

✎ Show the children 19 pairs of socks (have children each bring in a pair). Carefully count 19 pairs and announce, "I have counted 38 socks." When the children notice that you counted 19 pair and announced 38, explain that each pair has 2 socks. Skip count by 2's to 38. (Save the socks for another activity on Day 58.)

# Day 39

♥ Present this problem-solving activity to children: "If you eat 3 meals a day— breakfast, lunch, and dinner—how many meals would you eat in 13 days?" Provide paper plates and manipulatives for children to use as they solve the problem. If the children are comfortable with skip counting by 2's and 5's, lead them in skip counting from 1 to 39 by 3's.

## Celebrate 40 Day

### Supply List

| | |
|---|---|
| yarn | number cubes |
| copies of page 57 (1 per child) | red, yellow, and green crayons or markers |
| upholstery needles | plain white paper |
| 0-shaped cereal | variety of stamps and stamp pads |

Read
*Let's Count*
by Tana
Hoban

**Number Necklace:** Provide small bowls of cereal and a length of yarn or string for each child. As the children string exactly 40 pieces of cereal on the necklaces, note that the necklaces are getting longer. Later, children can eat the cereal.

Encourage children to copy Tana Hoban's pattern illustrated on her "40" page. Use Froot Loops® to alternately string 4 pieces of one color, changing to different colors until 40 pieces of cereal have been strung.

**Play:** Use the reproducible game-board to play "Shapes Lead to 40." Two to four children can play at a time. Each child rolls a number cube in turn and moves a small marker the indicated number of spaces.

**Do:** Give each child a copy of the "Shapes Lead to 40" reproducible. Instruct them to color the spaces in a pattern of 4's (4 red, 4 yellow, 4 green, and so on).

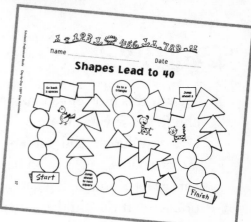

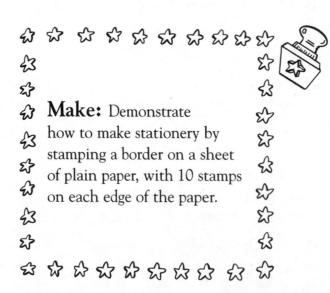

**Make:** Demonstrate how to make stationery by stamping a border on a sheet of plain paper, with 10 stamps on each edge of the paper.

## Days 41 - 49

### Supply List

copies of page 58
(1 per child)

calculators

pencils

"45 cents off" coupons

assortment of small items
in reclosable bags

47 marbles

49 stickers

**Vocabulary**

array

calculator

recording
sheet

**Read** *Miss
Bindergarten
Stays Home
From
Kindergarten*
by Joseph
Slate

### About Days 41-49

This section introduces the use of calculators to add numbers together, grocery coupons that represent a particular number, and recording sheets to note mathematical information. Continue to use the Hundred Chart so that children develop their understanding of the patterns of counting. Give children their own laminated Hundred Chart (page 54) and ask them to point to each number with a pencil during this week's daily count. Count by 1's every day, and on even numbered days, count by 2's.

## Day 41

Show the class the book *Miss Bindergarten Stays Home From Kindergarten.* Write the title of the book on chart paper and count the number of letters as you write. There are several ways to lead the class in counting the number of letters in the title. You can underline each letter as it is counted, use two colors of markers to alternately circle the letters, count the letters in each word (writing that number above the word and then adding the value of all the words together), or highlight alternate letters as you count.

# Day 42

Distribute calculators, pencils, and recording sheets (page 58). Ask children to begin by writing 3 in the first blank on the recording sheet. Then use the calculator to keep adding 3 to that beginning numeral, recording each new sum until they fill in all 14 blanks. Children should have 42 in the final blank.

# Day 43

Ask small groups of children to sort a bag of items (create several collections of 43 from an assortment of small items such as buttons, keys, nuts, bolts, pebbles, or coins and store them in gallon-sized reclosable bags), and then talk about their sorting strategies. Discuss how different number combinations all equal 43.

# Day 44

Using Unifix® cubes, build enough 10-cube rods and set aside enough singles to make 44. Count to 44. Model adding $11+11+11+11=44$.

Draw four football teams' formations with X's and O's (use the diagram on page 18 as a model). Ask children to count the number of players on each team with you. Model writing the twin number 44, and have children practice writing 44 in the air.

## Day 45

✏️ Pass out "45 cents off" coupons to all children. Discuss using coupons to save money at the grocery store. Have them estimate how many nickels are in 45 cents, and record the estimates. Then pass out reclosable bags of nickels, and help children use the nickels to count by 5's to 45.

## Day 46

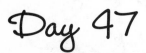

Line up 23 pairs of shoes within the circle area. Ask children to count how many individual shoes there are. Then, skip counting by 2's, count the pairs.

## Day 47

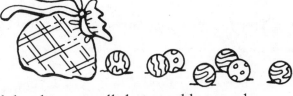

✏️ Present this problem to the children: "3 children are playing a game of marbles and decide to put all their marbles together. One has 14 marbles, another child has 16, and the other has 17. How many marbles will they use in the game?" Children can use marbles to act out the story.

Since all the children will want to take off their shoes for the Day 46 activity, you may have to adjust the activity to the number of children in your class. If you have more than 23 children, do the activity more than once. If you have fewer, borrow some children from another classroom!

## Day 48

⭐ Remind children about counting to 12 (1 dozen) from Day 12. Discuss how 4 dozen cookies would make 48. Children can count the cookies as you draw them on the board.

# Day 49

🐱 Draw a 7-by-7 grid on chart paper. As the children count with you, fill in each column in the array with a sticker until each square is filled. Explain that 7 groups of 7 make 49.

Empty paper towel and toilet paper rolls will be needed for an activity on the Celebrate 60 Day. Begin now to ask families to collect these and send them to school.

To help children who are not ready to count independently to 50, provide a container with 5 sections (such as an empty egg carton trimmed down to 5 sections). Have children count, placing 10 pieces of cereal in each of the 5 sections.

## Celebrate 50 Day

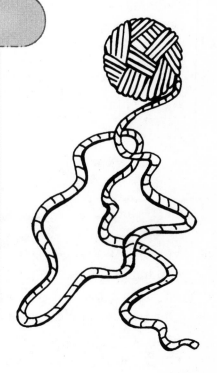

### Supply List

yarn

O-shaped cereal

upholstery needles

number cubes

pennies, nickels, dimes, and quarters

small self-adhesive stars

puzzles of the United States

copies of page 59 (1 per child)

## Number Necklace:

Provide small bowls of cereal and a length of yarn or string for each child. As the children string exactly 50 pieces of cereal on the necklaces, note that they will be "twice" as long on Day 100. Later, children can eat the cereal.

**Play:** Prepare reclosable bags that include 50 pennies, 10 nickels, 5 dimes, and 2 quarters. Many young children know that it takes 2 quarters to make 50 cents. Encourage children to create 50 cents in other coin combinations. Some children may simply match 25 pennies with 1 quarter, others may come up with multiple combinations.

**Do:** Give each child a copy of the American flag reproducible (page 59). Provide self-adhesive stars and encourage children to stick one star on each star on the flag. Help children make the connection between the reproducible and the real American flag in the classroom.

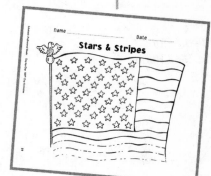

**Read:** Write the following poem on chart paper. Teach it to the children using echo reading, then choral reading. Chanting this poem will support children as they work on coin combinations to equal 50 cents.

**Buying a Soft Drink**

Fifty cents, Fifty cents,
I need to find just fifty cents.
Fifty cents, Fifty cents,
A soda costs just fifty cents.
Two quarters, Five dimes,
Ten nickels, That's fine.
Fifty cents, Fifty cents.
I need to find just fifty cents.

**Make:** Challenge children to work in groups to put together a 50-states puzzle. Remind children to compare shapes of the puzzle pieces to the picture on the puzzle box (or a map of the United States).

## Days 51 - 59

### Supply List

51 paper plates

book for each child
with at least 53 pages

Judy® Clock

digital clock

copies of page 58 and
60 (1 per child)

pairs of socks

calculators, pencils,
and recording sheets

analog clock

deck of cards

Read
*I Read Signs*
by Tana Hoban

**Vocabulary**

analog

digital

grid

hour

minutes

sum

### About Days 51-59

Most activities in this section reinforce previous concepts: solving problems, counting page numbers, using calculators, counting letters in familiar text, and counting pairs of socks. The familiarity of the activities helps children work with increasingly larger numbers. The new activities in this section relate to games (counting the cards in a deck and creating their own Bingo game with a reproducible grid) and also to reading a clock.

## Day 51

Present this problem to children: "If you eat three meals a day—breakfast, lunch, and dinner—how many meals would you eat in 51 days?" Provide paper plates and manipulatives for children to use as they solve the problem. Count by 3's after children arrive at the answer.

# Day 52

Show children a deck of playing cards and ask if anyone knows how many cards are in a deck. Then chorally count the cards as you turn them over one at a time, making 5 stacks of 10 (with an extra 2 cards left over). When writing the number 52, remind the class that 52 means 5 10's and 2 1's. (Remember to remove the Jokers before you start!)

# Day 53

Give each child a book. Count the pages 1-53, as children turn the pages.

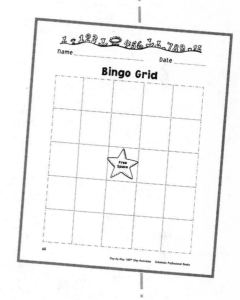

name _____ Date _____

**Bingo Grid**

Free Space

60

Day-by-Day 100th Day Activities    Scholastic Professional Books

# Day 54

Distribute Bingo Grids and invite children to fill the squares with any numbers they choose, using "54" up to 5 times. Randomly call out numbers as children cross them out, Bingo-style. The first child with 5 across wins.

# Day 55

Use *I Read Signs* to show speed limit signs. Hoban's photograph shows a "Speed Limit 15" sign. Discuss the fact that there are different speed limits for different parts of town. Indicate that the twin number 55 is the "speed limit of the day."

# Day 56

✏ Distribute calculators, pencils, and recording sheets (page 58). Ask children to write 4 in the first blank on the recording sheet, then use the calculator to keep adding 4 to the sum until they fill in all 14 blanks. Children should have 56 written in the final blank.

# Day 57

♥ Write the following nursery rhyme on chart paper. Ask children to count the letters in the rhyme:

Falling down,
Falling down.
London Bridge is
falling down,
My fair lady.

# Day 58

✏ Show children the previously collected pairs of socks. Carefully count 29 pairs and announce, "I have counted 58 socks." When the children notice that you counted 29 pair and announced 58, explain that each pair has 2 socks. Together, skip count by 2's to 58.

# Day 59

♥ Explain that there are 60 minutes in an hour. Schedule the discussion about "counting up to 100" so that children can observe a digital clock at 1 minute to the hour. That way, they can see 8:59 or 9:59 and watch the time change to the hour. Use a Judy® clock (or teacher-created analog clock) and move the minute hand slowly as you lead children in counting from 1 to 59.

## Celebrate 60 Day

### Supply List

| | |
|---|---|
| yarn | scissors |
| 0-shaped cereal | copies of page 61 (1 per child) |
| upholstery needles | masking tape |
| empty paper towel or toilet paper rolls | |

**Number Necklace:** Provide small bowls of cereal and a length of yarn or string for each child. Challenge children to string exactly 60 pieces of cereal on the necklace. Later, the children can eat the cereal.

**Do:** Use the reproducible "Stars" (page 61) to count the points in each star (5) and in all the stars (60). If children can write the numerals 1-60, have them label each point of the stars.

Read *Just a Minute* by Teddy Slater

Cut the yarn between 24 and 36 inches long for these larger numbers. This prevents the cereal from rubbing on the child's neck. After the child strings the cereal, you can adjust the length when the knot is tied, eliminating any excess.

**Make:** Challenge the children to make a rod that is exactly 60 inches long. Provide empty paper towel and toilet paper rolls, scissors, and masking tape for each group of children. At various points around the room, place masking tape that is 60 inches long so children can measure their creations. Ask children to tape the empty rolls together until they reach 60 inches.

Or, as a class, bake 60 cookies as an example of 5 dozen!

## Days 61 - 69

### Supply List

| | |
|---|---|
| calculators | assortment of small items |
| Place Value Chart (page 62) | box of 64 crayons |
| cubes | nickels |
| toy cars | plastic forks, spoons, and knives (21 of each) |

### About Days 61-69

Numbers this large may be challenging for some children. For this reason, the activities in this section build on earlier concepts. You may want to use a highlighter on the Hundred Chart for multiples of 3 to reinforce the idea of skip counting by 3's.

# Day 61

Give each child a calculator. Remind everyone to listen carefully and push only the buttons that you tell them to push. Call out "9 + 12 + 15 + 25" (or any other number combination that totals 61). If all children do not get the total of 61 on the calculator, repeat the equation and have them try again.

# Day 62

Ask small groups of children to sort a bag of items (create several collections of 62 from an assortment of small items like buttons, keys, nuts, bolts, pebbles, or coins and store them in gallon-sized reclosable bags) then talk about their sorting strategies. Lead children into a discussion about how different number combinations can add up to 62.

# Day 63

Show a collection of 63 plastic utensils (21 forks, 21 spoons, 21 knives). Count the utensils. Then sort them by type of utensil, counting out the small groups. Finally, sort them by table setting, then count by 3's.

# Day 64

Display a new box of 64 crayons. Take them out of the box one at a time and place them on the floor in groups of 10. As you place the crayons on the floor, lead the children in counting from 1 to 64. Then count them again by 10's, then 1's: 10, 20, 30, 40, 50, 60, 61, 62, 63, 64.

# Day 65

Give pairs of children reclosable bags containing 13 nickels and help them count by 5's to 65.

# Day 66

Using Unifix® cubes, build enough 10-block rods and singles to make 66. Count to 66. Model adding 11+11+11+11+11+11=66.

Draw 6 football teams' formations with X's and O's. Ask children to count the number of players on each team with you. Model writing the twin number 66, and have children practice writing 66 in the air.

# Day 67

Count the letters in the nursery rhyme "The Farmer in the Dell":

> The farmer in the dell,
> The farmer in the dell,
> Hi-ho, the derry-o,
> The farmer in the dell.

# Day 68

Put 17 toy cars in the middle of the circle. Count the wheels on the cars together, from 1 to 68.

# Day 69

Present this problem: "If irises have 3 petals each, and you count 69 petals in a bouquet of irises, how many separate irises do you have?" Draw irises on chart paper to help children solve the problem. Count by 3's after arriving at the answer.

## Celebrate 70 Day

Read
*From One
to One
Hundred*
by Teri Sloat

### Supply List

| | |
|---|---|
| yarn | copies of page 62 (1 per child) |
| 0-shaped cereal | 70 blocks per pair of builders |
| upholstery needles | paper plates |
| number cubes | 70 small objects per pair of players |

**Number Necklace:** Provide small bowls of cereal and a length of yarn or string for each child. Challenge children to string exactly 70 pieces of cereal on the necklace. Later, children can eat the cereal.

**Play:** Change the game "20's" to the game of "70's." Each pair of players needs a paper plate, 70 small objects, and a number cube (these items store easily in a gallon-sized reclosable bag). The first player rolls, then moves that number of objects onto the plate. The other player rolls, adding that number of objects to the plate. Play continues until 70 objects are on the plate. You can also play with two number cubes, making the game go faster.

**Do:** Ask children to color the houses on the reproducible page, counting from 1 to 70. They can use a different color for each group of houses.

**Make:** Provide pairs of children with 70 blocks each. Challenge them to build a block structure with only those blocks. Photograph children with their block creations, hanging the photos, with child-created labels, on a bulletin board.

## Days 71-79

### Supply List

| | |
|---|---|
| calculators | quarters |
| 1-inch blocks | Unifix® cubes |
| yardsticks | recording of "76 Trombones" |
| books with at least 73 pages | paper plates and manipulatives |
| 100 chart (page 54) | Place Value Chart (page 63) |

**Vocabulary**

place value

### About Days 71-79

The new math concept presented in this section is "place value," using the Place Value Chart. Repeat this activity as often as the class needs it to understand the concept of 10's and 1's place values.

## Day 71

Provide a calculator for each child. Remind everyone to listen carefully and push only the buttons that you tell them to push. Call out "20 + 10 + 15 + 25 + 1" (or any other number combination that totals 71). If all children do not get the total of 71 on the calculator, help them try again.

# Day 72

⭐ Remind children of the Day 36 activity of measuring a yardstick with 1-inch blocks. Have them estimate how many 1-inch blocks it would take to measure 2 yardsticks (remind them that a yardstick is 36 inches). Record the numbers estimated. Then ask 2 children to make a line of blocks parallel to the yardstick. Help the class count aloud as each block is added. Finally, see which estimate was closest.

✏ Use 72 cookies as an example of 6 dozen.

> Cut a colored, transparent report cover into small squares to highlight the numbers on a Hundreds Pocket Chart. These pieces slip easily between the number card and the clear pocket.

# Day 73

⭐ Give each child a copy of a book with at least 73 pages. Count the pages 1 to 73 aloud, as children turn the pages.

# Day 74

✏ Color all the even numbers on a Hundred Chart up to 74 with a highlighter. Point to the even numbers, and count by 2's to 74.

# Day 75

⭐ Show children 3 quarters. Count 25, 50, 75. Explain that 3 quarters is $\frac{3}{4}$ of a dollar. Then count pennies and nickels to 75.

# Day 76

✏ Play a recording of "76 Trombones" from the musical *The Music Man*. Ask children to march in place as they count from 1 to 76.

# Day 77

☆ Using Unifix® cubes, build enough 10-block rods and singles to make 77. Count to 77. Model adding 11+11+11+11+11+11+11=77.

✏ Draw 7 football teams' formations with X's and O's. Ask children to count the number of players on each team with you. Model writing the twin number 77, and have children practice writing 77 in the air.

# Day 78

☆ Present this problem: "If you eat 3 meals a day—breakfast, lunch, and dinner—how many meals would you eat in 26 days?" Provide paper plates and manipulatives for the children to use as they solve the problem. Count by 3's after they arrive at the answer.

> Children can use cubes to represent breakfast, lunch, and dinner on paper plates

# Day 79

✏ Using a Place Value Chart (page 63) and Unifix® cubes, model counting from 1-79, snapping cubes together each time you reach a multiple of 10 and moving the rod into the 10's place on the chart. Repeat the count of the 79 cubes by counting by 10's to 70, then by 1's to 79.

## Celebrate 80 Day

Read
*Ready or Not,
Here I Come!*
by Teddy
Slater

### Supply List

yarn

O-shaped cereal

posterboard (1 sheet
for every 4 children)

upholstery needles

several collections of 80 buttons,
keys, nuts, pebbles, or coins

**Number Necklace:** Provide small bowls of cereal and a length of yarn or string for each child. Challenge children to string exactly 80 pieces of cereal on the necklace. Later, children can eat the cereal.

**Play:** From an assortment of small items such as buttons, keys, nuts, bolts, pebbles, or coins, create several collections of 80, storing them in gallon-sized reclosable bags. Ask small groups of children to sort a bag of items and record their sorting strategies. Come together as a group and record the different strategies on chart paper. Lead children in a discussion about how different number combinations can equal 80.

**Do:** On a Hundred Chart, have children color the numbers 5, 10, 15, 20, 25, 30, 35, 40, 45, 50, 55, 60, 65, 70, 75, and 80. Then direct them to circle the numbers 10, 20, 30, 40, 50, 60, 70, and 80. Children can then use their chart to count by 5s and 10s.

**Make:** Ask children to brainstorm a list of small things they can easily draw—squares, triangles, circles, rectangles, stars, flowers, trees, and so on. Give each group of 4 students a posterboard, and explain that each child in the group should draw 2 different sets of 10 things. Display posterboards with the title: "8 Sets of 10 Equal 80."

## Days 81 - 89

### Supply List

| | |
|---|---|
| calculators | 17 nickels per pair of children |
| pencils | recording sheets (page 58) |
| highlighters | reclosable bags |
| 81 stickers | |

### About Days 81-89

Most of the activities in this section are familiar activities, changed only by using larger numbers. The new activities are counting the keys of a piano and finding the number 89 in grocery circulars. Any of these activities can be replaced with ideas from Days 21-29.

## Day 81

 Draw a 9-by-9 grid on the board. As children count with you, fill in each column in the array with a sticker until each square is filled.

## Day 82

 Write the following nursery rhyme on chart paper. Count the letters :

Star light, star bright,
First star I see tonight,
I wish I may, I wish I might,
Have the wish I wish tonight.

Gather enough grocery store circulars for each child in your class to use on Day 89 (make sure that at least one item is priced at 89 cents). newspaper ads can be used as well.

# Day 83

Distribute calculators. Remind children to listen carefully and push only the buttons that you tell them to push. Call out "22 + 16 + 34 + 11" (or any other number combination that totals 83). If all children do not get the total 83 on the calculator, help them try again.

# Day 84

Distribute calculators, pencils, and recording sheets (page 58). Ask them to begin by writing 6 in the first blank on the recording sheet. Then have them use the calculator to keep adding 6 to that beginning numeral, recording each new sum until they fill in all 14 blanks. See how many children have 84 in the final blank.

Use 84 cookies as an example of 7 dozen.

# Day 85

Give pairs of children reclosable bags containing 17 nickels. Help them count by 5's to 85.

# Day 86

Color all the even numbers on a Hundred Chart up to 86 with highlighter. Point to the even numbers, and count by 2's to 86.

# Day 87

Present this problem: "Each iris has 3 petals. You have 29 irises in a bouquet. How many separate iris petals are in the bouquet?" Provide manipulatives for the children to use as they solve the problem. Count by 3's after they arrive at the answer.

# Day 88

If there is a piano available, play each key as the children count from 1 to 88. If a piano is not available, show a picture of a piano and count in unison from 1 to 88, or tape yourself playing each key on a piano while counting the keys. (A parent or another teacher might make the tape at home.)

# Day 89

Write the number 89. Pass out grocery circulars and highlighters and have children highlight all the 89-cent items they can find.

## Celebrate 90 Day

### Supply List

| | |
|---|---|
| yarn | reclosable bags |
| 0-shaped cereal | copies of page 64 (1 per child) |
| upholstery needles | paper clips (1 box per child) |
| bowl of popcorn | |

Read
*From One to One Hundred*
by Teri Sloat

**Number Necklace:** Provide small bowls of cereal and a length of yarn or string for each child. Challenge children to string exactly 90 pieces of cereal on the necklace. Later, children can eat the cereal.

**Play:** Ask children to take a handful of popcorn each from a bowl. Post 9 reclosable bags on a bulletin board. Children can work together to put 10 pieces in each bag until the collection reaches 90. Count them together as a class (by 10's, then by 5's, and then by 1's).

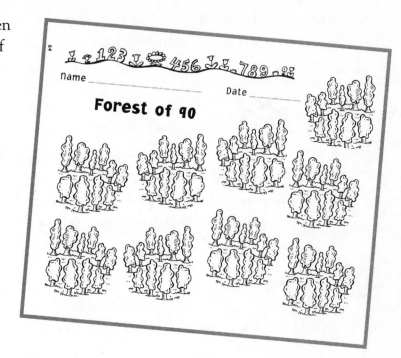

**Do:** Distribute copies of page 64. Ask children to color 10 trees in one color, 10 in another color, and so on, until all the trees are colored.

**Make:** Give pairs of children a box of paper clips each and invite them to link 90 paper clips together.

## Days 91-99

### Supply List

| | |
|---|---|
| Place Value Chart (page 63) | nickels |
| calculators | 23 toy cars |
| Unifix® cubes | Hundred Chart |
| books with at least 97 pages (one per child) | plastic utensils: 33 forks, 33 spoons, and 33 knives |
| highlighter | |

### About Days 91-99

You are nearing the end!  You can choose from among the suggestions offered, and add any other activities you've found to be successful.

**Vocabulary**

flat

rod

unit

## Day 91

Using a Place Value Chart (page 63) and Unifix® cubes, model counting from 1 to 91, snapping cubes together each time you reach a multiple of 10 and moving the rod into the 10's place on the chart.  Repeat the count of the 91 cubes by counting by 10's to 90, then by 1's to 91.

## Day 92

Count the number of wheels on 23 toy cars.

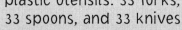

# Day 93

Provide a calculator for each child. Remind children to listen carefully and push only the buttons that you tell them to push. Call out "22 + 16 + 34 + 21" (or any other number combination that totals 93). If all children do not get the total of 93 on the calculator, help them try again.

# Day 94

Write the following nursery rhyme on the board. Count the letters in the rhyme:

It's raining, it's pouring;
The old man is snoring.
Bumped his head
And he went to bed
And he couldn't get up in the morning.

# Day 95

Give pairs of children reclosable bags containing 19 nickels each. Help them count by 5's to 95. Have them predict how many more nickels are needed to make a dollar!

# Day 96

Remind children about counting by the dozens. Draw 8-dozen cookies on the board as the children count them with you.

# Day 97

✎ Give each child a book with at least 97 pages. Count the pages 1 to 97 aloud, as children turn the pages.

# Day 98

♥ Color all the even numbers on a Hundred Chart up to 98 with highlighter. Point to the even numbers, and count by 2's to 98.

# Day 99

✎ Offer a collection of 99 plastic utensils (33 forks, 33 spoons, and 33 knives). Count the utensils. Then sort them, counting them in 3 groups.

*And, finally . . .*

## Celebrate 100 Day!

### Supply List

| | |
|---|---|
| yarn | tempera paint |
| ball | Base 10® units, rods, and flats |
| upholstery needles | 10 empty plastic soft-drink bottles |
| music | small assorted snack foods |
| timer | 100-piece jigsaw puzzles |
| 0-shaped cereal | blank paper |
| fabric paint | assorted rubber stamps |

### Number Necklace:

Provide small bowls of cereal and a length of yarn or string for each child. Challenge children to string exactly 100 pieces of cereal on the necklace. Later, children can eat the cereal!

### Play:

Dance for 100 seconds! Brainstorm other activities that can be done for 100 seconds and try them, too.

"Bowl for 100" using empty soft-drink bottles labeled by 10's, 10 to 100. Place the bottles in a line in numerical order, with a small space between each bottle. Roll a ball at the 10 bottle until it falls. Counting by 10's, roll a ball at each bottle until all 10 bottles have fallen. (To make the game harder, fill the bottles partially with sand, or mix the order of the bottles in the line.)

### Do:

Make 100 handprints for a bulletin board. Use tempera paint in various colors.

On a piece of paper, children can collect signatures until they reach 100.

Complete 100-piece jigsaw puzzles.

## Read:

Read *Emily's First 100 Days of School* by Rosemary Wells. In it, Emily leaves for school on day 1, continuing her adventures at school until day 100's celebrations.

Read *Fluffy's 100th Day at School* by Kate McMullan. Three short stories illustrate how Ms. Day's class celebrates the 100th day of school with their guinea pig, Fluffy.

Read Trudy Harris's book, *100 Days of School*. This clever "what if" book appeals to young children's sense of humor with its rhyming questions and answers about 100.

Read *100th Day Worries* by Margery Cuyler. Children will identify with Jessica's worries about what to bring to school for her 100th-day collection.

## Make:

Create a T-shirt that illustrates 100 items! Children can stamp an image 100 times, use fabric paint or attach collections of 100 items to the shirt (safety pins, buttons, ribbon loops, pom-poms, and so on).

Write and illustrate "The 100 People Book." Children can draw pictures of family members, school helpers, and friends until they have 100 people. Bind the pages together with a title page.

For the day's snack, make Gorp, a mixture of high-energy foods. Have children count out 10 treats from 10 bowls of small snack foods (such as cheese puffs, M&Ms®, marshmallows, raisins, cereal, nuts, caramel corn, dried fruit, popcorn, and so on), then place them in a small reclosable bag. Or, provide each child with a Hundred Chart (page 54) and ask everyone to place one bit of food on each number until they reach 100.

# Hundred Chart

| 1 | 2 | 3 | 4 | 5 | 6 | 7 | 8 | 9 | 10 |
|---|---|---|---|---|---|---|---|---|----|
| 11 | 12 | 13 | 14 | 15 | 16 | 17 | 18 | 19 | 20 |
| 21 | 22 | 23 | 24 | 25 | 26 | 27 | 28 | 29 | 30 |
| 31 | 32 | 33 | 34 | 35 | 36 | 37 | 38 | 39 | 40 |
| 41 | 42 | 43 | 44 | 45 | 46 | 47 | 48 | 49 | 50 |
| 51 | 52 | 53 | 54 | 55 | 56 | 57 | 58 | 59 | 60 |
| 61 | 62 | 63 | 64 | 65 | 66 | 67 | 68 | 69 | 70 |
| 71 | 72 | 73 | 74 | 75 | 76 | 77 | 78 | 79 | 80 |
| 81 | 82 | 83 | 84 | 85 | 86 | 87 | 88 | 89 | 90 |
| 91 | 92 | 93 | 94 | 95 | 96 | 97 | 98 | 99 | 100 |

Day-by-Day 100th Day Activities   Scholastic Professional Books

Name _____          Date _____

# Wheels

_____

*Scholastic Professional Books*   **Day-by-Day 100th Day Activities**

Name _____

Date _____

# Lights

_____

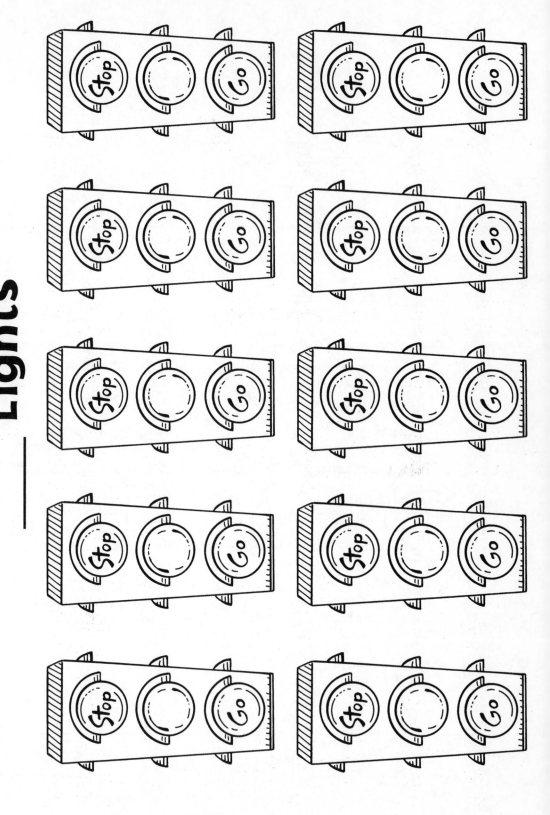

Name _____

Date _____

# Shapes Lead to 40

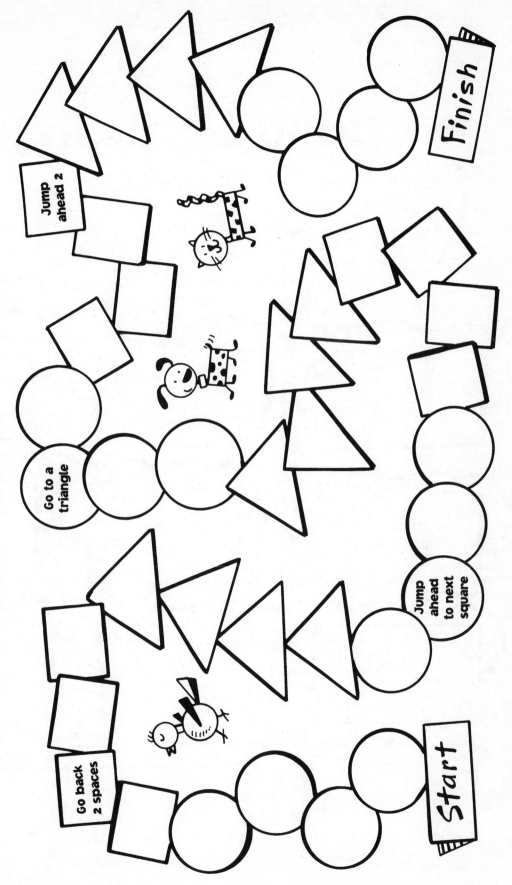

On the game board: Finish, Start, Jump ahead 2, Go to a triangle, Jump ahead to next square, Go back 2 spaces

57

Name _____ Date _____

# Using a Calculator

Name _____

Date _____

# Stars & Stripes

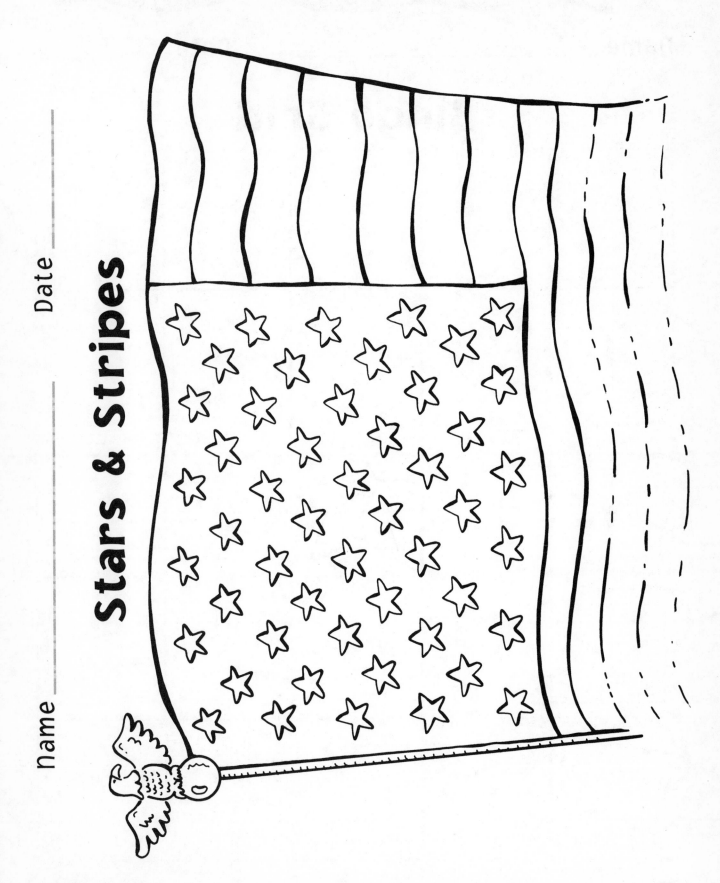

*Scholastic Professional Books*   Day-by-Day 100th Day Activities

Name _____ Date _____

# Bingo Grid

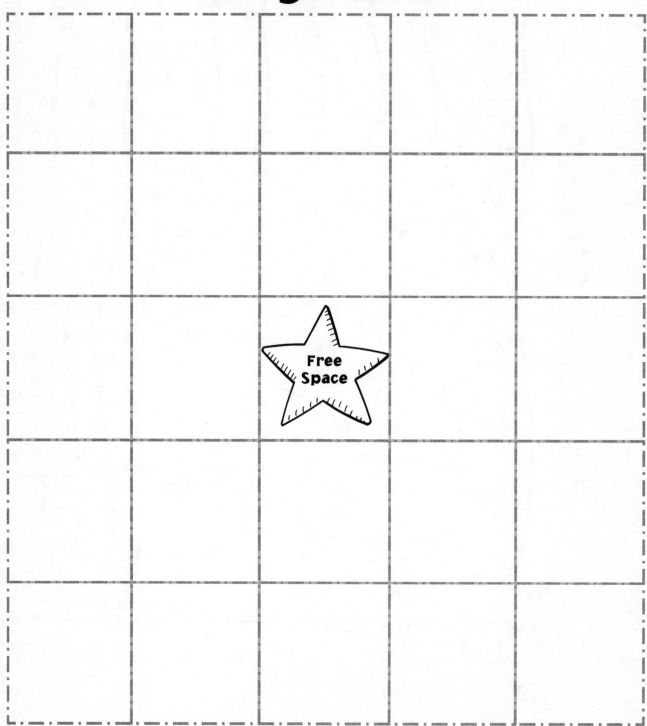

Free
Space

Name _____     Date _____

# Stars

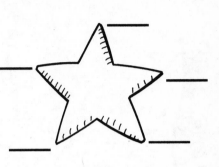

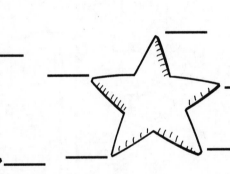

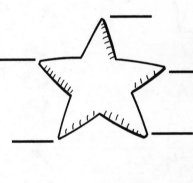

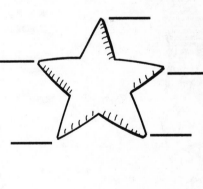

*Scholastic Professional Books*     *Day-by-Day 100th Day Activities*

Name _____

Date _____

# 70 Houses

# Place Value Chart

| Hundreds | Tens | Ones |
| --- | --- | --- |
|  |  |  |

*Scholastic Professional Books*   Day-by-Day 100th Day Activities

Name

Date

# Forest of 90

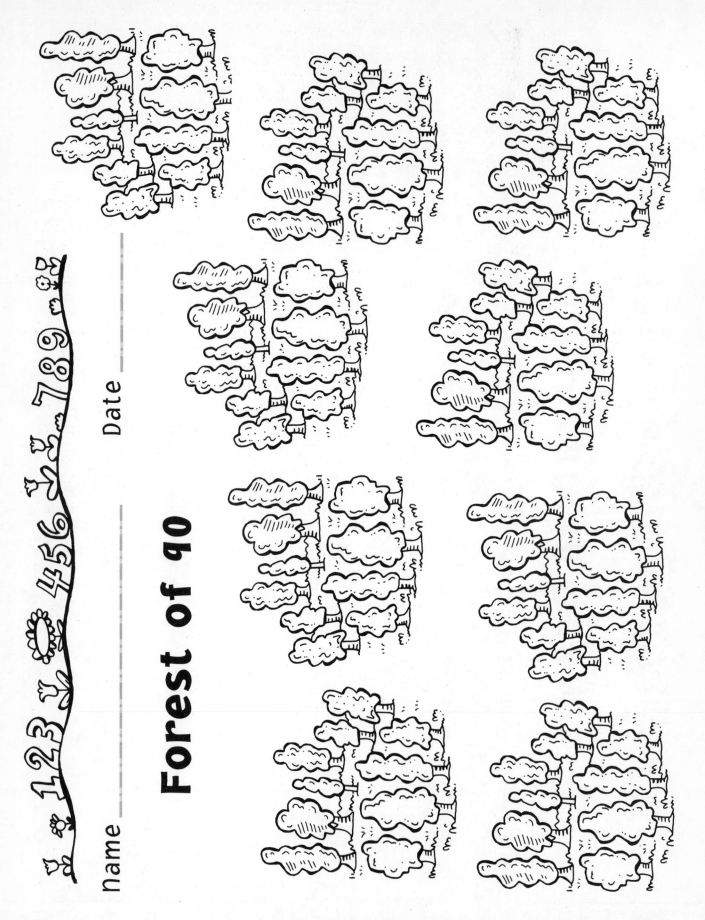

Day-by-Day 100th Day Activities    Scholastic Professional Books